WISDOM
FROM THE
WHITEBOARD

Foreword

I am one of those people you hear about who could not get pregnant. It took me 7 years and hundreds of fertility shots, and finally, on February 8, 2003, Katelyn Clare Reed was born. She was a 7-pound 13-ounce, pink skinned, black-haired cutie who also happens to have Down Syndrome. *

Despite Katelyn's surprise diagnosis, we fell instantly in love with our sweet baby girl. And we were terrified. This was a challenge for which no one and nothing could prepare us. Those first 24 hours were a complete blur, but once the fog parted, we were able to find some hope and strength. Through the help of faith, family, friends, and our brilliant Down Syndrome Community, we found our way.

What I know for sure is that at 19 years of age at the writing of this book, Katelyn has seldom allowed her diagnosis to sway her from accomplishing her dreams. She has been professionally acting since she was 4 years old (check her out on IMDB), she is a first-degree black belt, a downhill skier, she has been in over 30 community musical theater productions, she has been in a competitive show choir for 6 years, and she is an avid writer, traveler, music buff and a devoted "Gleek" for all you *Glee* fans out there. Perhaps the most remarkable thing about Katelyn is her ability to persevere despite her challenges and maintain a positive attitude in a world that is not always kind to those with special needs.

This book is the result of a 3-year practice of attempting to understand her own thoughts and feelings and finding a way to survive in a world that can feel harsh for the differently abled. It all began in 2018 when Katelyn was preparing to start high school and her Papa was diagnosed with terminal cancer. I noticed that her nighttime routine got a little longer because she started writing quotes on her giant whiteboard. I was inspired by her creativity and assumed she would lose steam eventually, but it continued. Her wisdom became deeper and very much tied to the feelings, experiences, and observations of her life and the world around her. It became like a meditation that allowed the loud world to fade away and gave her space to sort through her thoughts and chart a course for the next day. We started to share some of her best quotes with friends and family who were touched by her words. Several asked if they could use her quotes to motivate their own kids, families, and colleagues. Eventually, we coined her nightly practice, "Wisdom from the Whiteboard."

Many have asked if Katelyn would compile her whiteboard writings into a book, and here we are. Her desire to share herself and have deep compassion for the health and well-being of others has become her mission and passion.

I hope you enjoy her work as much as we have enjoyed seeing this project evolve.

With love and gratitude,

Kelly Reed

---

* Down Syndrome or trisomy 21 is a genetic disability that deposits an extra 21st chromosome into every cell of a person's body. What this means for each individual spans a wide spectrum. It is considered an intellectual disability that is most often accompanied by low muscle tone, heart defects, and myriad other physical maladies and mental challenges. Down syndrome occurs in roughly 1 in 800 births.

Message From the Author

Dear Reader,

You may not know this, but I have Down Syndrome. All my life I have felt alone and different. Sometimes, I would shut myself off and be ashamed of who I am, but I learned over time that I am not alone because I have people who I look up to who love me even though I am different. What I want you to know is that you are not alone either. There are people in your life who love and trust YOU and that is enough. Friends may come and go but remember, each of our journey's is unique; no journey looks the same. Your own personal life is different than mine, but I know you have challenges just like I do. I have learned that as you move forward through your life, it helps to look for hope. It also helps to refuse to allow people to tear you down. You are special and God made you exactly the right way. Trust this, believe, and do not doubt yourself. There will always be people on your path who make you feel stuck or less than. Have the courage to boost yourself up. Be your own best fan.

I wrote these quotes to help me and now to help you, too. I want you to believe that you have a place to come and feel safe and welcome. Come to these pages when you are feeling alone, or stuck, or blocked, or doubting yourself. This journal will be a place to be inspired: write, feel it all, color it out, and get some good advice for how to handle life when things get hard. Best of luck on your journey.

Katelyn Reed

Dedicated to Andrew Babbitt, the best counselor, mentor, and role model a girl could have.

CONTENTS

COURAGE

cour-age /kerij/ noun -

The ability to do something meaningful even though it frightens you. To have strength in the face of pain or grief.

QUOTES ABOUT COURAGE

Reflect

What is a hard thing in your life?
What is one step you could take to make
it a little better?

_____
_____
_____
_____
_____
_____
_____
_____
_____
_____
_____
_____
_____
_____
_____
_____
_____
_____
_____
_____
_____
_____
_____
_____
_____
_____
_____
_____

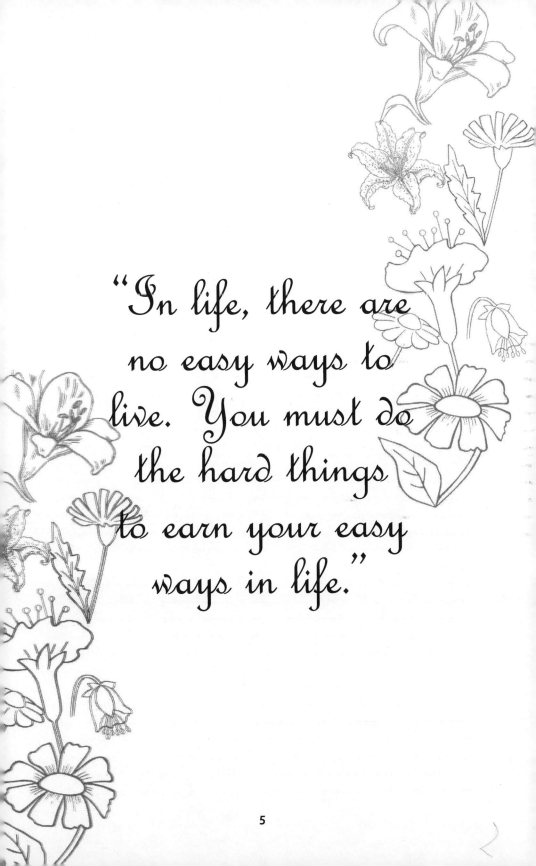

"In life, there are no easy ways to live. You must do the hard things to earn your easy ways in life."

Reflect

What is the next best choice you can make for yourself? Be honest.

_____
_____
_____
_____
_____
_____
_____
_____
_____
_____
_____
_____
_____
_____
_____
_____
_____
_____
_____
_____
_____
_____
_____
_____
_____
_____
_____

"Make good choices and be honest. There are some challenges you must deal with, but someone like you can push through it!"

Reflect

In your heart, what is it that you truly wish to express out loud in the world?

_____
_____
_____
_____
_____
_____
_____
_____
_____
_____
_____
_____
_____
_____
_____
_____
_____
_____
_____
_____
_____
_____
_____
_____
_____
_____
_____
_____

"This is the day when you take a breath and express yourself out there. Show the world what you can do!"

Reflect

So, what do YOU believe in?
What do YOU know for sure?

_____
_____
_____
_____
_____
_____
_____
_____
_____
_____
_____
_____
_____
_____
_____
_____
_____
_____
_____
_____
_____
_____
_____
_____
_____
_____
_____
_____
_____

"Whatever you do, always stand up for what you believe in."

Reflect

What have you failed at recently?
How did it feel? Did you learn
something valuable about yourself?

_____

_____

_____

_____

_____

_____

_____

_____

_____

_____

_____

_____

_____

_____

_____

_____

_____

_____

_____

_____

_____

_____

_____

_____

_____

_____

_____

"If you fail at something, all you can do is try again. If you do can do that, you will eventually succeed."

Reflect

What can you do differently today that did not work out so great for you within the last week or month?

_____
_____
_____
_____
_____
_____
_____
_____
_____
_____
_____
_____
_____
_____
_____
_____
_____
_____
_____
_____
_____
_____
_____
_____
_____
_____
_____
_____
_____
_____

"It is never too late to start over. If you were not happy about yesterday, try something different today."

Reflect

Is there something you have been aching
to try but are too scared?
Name it here. Try it!

_____
_____
_____
_____
_____
_____
_____
_____
_____
_____
_____
_____
_____
_____
_____
_____
_____
_____
_____
_____
_____
_____
_____
_____
_____
_____
_____
_____
_____

"Never stop
improving and
giving yourself
more challenges."

Reflect

What is bugging you that needs to be addressed? Can you tell one person about it today? Who?

_____
_____
_____
_____
_____
_____
_____
_____
_____
_____
_____
_____
_____
_____
_____
_____
_____
_____
_____
_____
_____
_____
_____
_____
_____
_____
_____
_____
_____

"If you know
something is wrong,
stand up for yourself,
say something,
and use your voice
to be heard."

19

Reflect

What is the personal cost of getting what you want without being true to yourself?

_____
_____
_____
_____
_____
_____
_____
_____
_____
_____
_____
_____
_____
_____
_____
_____
_____
_____
_____
_____
_____
_____
_____
_____
_____

"If you have a choice between being honest and just getting what you want, be honest."

Reflect

What is your most embarrassing weakness?
Now, what is your greatest strength?

_____
_____
_____
_____
_____
_____
_____
_____
_____
_____
_____
_____
_____
_____
_____
_____
_____
_____
_____
_____
_____
_____
_____
_____
_____
_____
_____
_____

"Don't let your
weaknesses define
who you are. Let
your strength be your
best friend. Always
try to be a better
person every day."

Reflect

Can you think of a time when you did something amazing even though it scared you to death? How did it feel?

_____
_____
_____
_____
_____
_____
_____
_____
_____
_____
_____
_____
_____
_____
_____
_____
_____
_____
_____
_____
_____
_____
_____
_____
_____
_____
_____
_____

"If you think you can do something, but you are afraid, just go for it! At the end of the day, you will thank yourself for doing it anyway!"

Reflect

Do you have one or two people you trust to ask for help? Who are they?

_____
_____
_____
_____
_____
_____
_____
_____
_____
_____
_____
_____
_____
_____
_____
_____
_____
_____
_____
_____
_____
_____
_____
_____
_____
_____
_____

"If you know you are struggling with something, don't hold back. Ask for help until you get the help you need. It will be worth it."

Reflect

What is a risk that you would love to take
if only you had the courage to take it?
Can you tell a trusted friend about it?

_____
_____
_____
_____
_____
_____
_____
_____
_____
_____
_____
_____
_____
_____
_____
_____
_____
_____
_____
_____
_____
_____
_____
_____
_____
_____
_____
_____
_____
_____

"Don't stay in your own pathway your whole life. Step out of your comfort zone."

Reflect

Make a list of 5 things you have always wanted to try. Pick one and plan to do it with no attachment to the outcome.

"Promise yourself
that you will be more
open-minded and
try new things."

Reflect

Failure is just information filled with lessons.
Think of a recent failure. What did you
learn about yourself that was positive?

_____
_____
_____
_____
_____
_____
_____
_____
_____
_____
_____
_____
_____
_____
_____
_____
_____
_____
_____
_____
_____
_____
_____
_____
_____
_____
_____

"Keep fighting hard to earn your success. If you fail, keep at it until you find your way."

Reflect

What do you think about a lot that just might change the world for the better?

_____
_____
_____
_____
_____
_____
_____
_____
_____
_____
_____
_____
_____
_____
_____
_____
_____
_____
_____
_____
_____
_____
_____
_____
_____
_____

"Tell the world what you believe. Your opinions matter right now. Don't let people silence you because what you have to offer may just change the world."

Reflect

What challenge are you facing in your life right now? Can you find a little hope and keep going?

_____
_____
_____
_____
_____
_____
_____
_____
_____
_____
_____
_____
_____
_____
_____
_____
_____
_____
_____
_____
_____
_____
_____
_____
_____
_____
_____
_____
_____

"All you need to do
in life is hope for the
best, stay positive,
and do your part.
This too shall pass."

Reflect

In what area of your life can you practice
a bit more independence? How would it
make a difference?

_____
_____
_____
_____
_____
_____
_____
_____
_____
_____
_____
_____
_____
_____
_____
_____
_____
_____
_____
_____
_____
_____
_____
_____
_____
_____
_____

"Believe that you can do things on your own."

39

Reflect

In what area of your life could you benefit by taking more of a leadership position? How can your unique perspective change things for the better?

_____
_____
_____
_____
_____
_____
_____
_____
_____
_____
_____
_____
_____
_____
_____
_____
_____
_____
_____
_____
_____
_____
_____
_____
_____
_____
_____
_____
_____

"Be a leader, not a follower. You will never know what it will be like to step up and take charge unless you do it."

What do you do when you are stressed?

_____
_____
_____
_____
_____
_____
_____
_____
_____
_____
_____
_____
_____
_____
_____
_____
_____
_____
_____
_____
_____
_____
_____
_____
_____

ASK
KATELYN

What do you do when you are stressed?

I make a hot cup of tea (chamomile or chai), I grab a cozy blanket, and watch an episode of a favorite show. I love *Glee*.

I go into my room, close the door, crank up the music, and sing and dance it out!

I freak out for a bit and then I talk to my mom, my aunt, or a trusted friend.

44

FAITH

faith /fāTH/ noun

to trust or believe in something

very strongly; to have complete

confidence in someone or

something.

QUOTES ABOUT FAITH

Reflect

What is your heart telling YOU to do?

_____
_____
_____
_____
_____
_____
_____
_____
_____
_____
_____
_____
_____
_____
_____
_____
_____
_____
_____
_____
_____
_____
_____
_____
_____
_____
_____
_____

"Let your heart
tell you what to
do in life."

Reflect

Who are your trusted people?

_____
_____
_____
_____
_____
_____
_____
_____
_____
_____
_____
_____
_____
_____
_____
_____
_____
_____
_____
_____
_____
_____
_____
_____
_____
_____
_____
_____

"You have people
to guide you
through the dark
times, trust that."

Reflect

What dream do you have for yourself?

"When you open your eyes in the morning, believe that everything you wish for will come true."

Reflect

Do YOU see the beauty in yourself?
List 5 things that are beautiful about
you in mind, body, and spirit.

_____
_____
_____
_____
_____
_____
_____
_____
_____
_____
_____
_____
_____
_____
_____
_____
_____
_____
_____
_____
_____
_____
_____
_____
_____
_____
_____
_____
_____
_____

"What God sees in you is a beautiful and lovely person. Do not let other people take you for granted."

Reflect

Do you feel in your soul that you truly belong here? Reflect.

_____
_____
_____
_____
_____
_____
_____
_____
_____
_____
_____
_____
_____
_____
_____
_____
_____
_____
_____
_____
_____
_____
_____
_____
_____
_____
_____

"In my inner self,
I always feel that
I belong here.
No matter what
happens in life, I
have my friends and
family plus God to
keep me safe."

Reflect

Do you have the courage to listen and apply God's guidance to your life?

_____
_____
_____
_____
_____
_____
_____
_____
_____
_____
_____
_____
_____
_____
_____
_____
_____
_____
_____
_____
_____
_____
_____
_____
_____
_____
_____
_____
_____

"If you believe that God is willing to give you guidance in life then you will have a fulfilling life ahead of you."

Reflect

Think of a time when you felt lonely with
no one to talk to and write about it.

"At times when you feel lonely and you have no one to talk to, ask God for help."

Reflect

How might you change your little corner of the world? Think BIG!

"If you think that you are not chosen or not enough, know that you are chosen to be here every day by God. He knows that you have it in you to change the world!"

Reflect

What steps forward have you taken in your life lately that make you feel proud?

_____
_____
_____
_____
_____
_____
_____
_____
_____
_____
_____
_____
_____
_____
_____
_____
_____
_____
_____
_____
_____
_____
_____
_____
_____
_____
_____
_____
_____
_____

"God created you to be an amazing human being. So, take that and create a person who is smart, loving, and can do anything you put your mind to. At the end of the day, you will be proud that you found your way."

Reflect

How can you allow your people to
support you more meaningfully?

_____
_____
_____
_____
_____
_____
_____
_____
_____
_____
_____
_____
_____
_____
_____
_____
_____
_____
_____
_____
_____
_____
_____
_____
_____
_____
_____
_____
_____

"The beautiful thing about life is that no matter where you go, you will always have people that love and support you along the way. Let them."

Reflect

What is something you dream of doing? Could you take a step or two toward your dream?

_____
_____
_____
_____
_____
_____
_____
_____
_____
_____
_____
_____
_____
_____
_____
_____
_____
_____
_____
_____
_____
_____
_____
_____
_____
_____

"Your dreams are
your deep thoughts
about your future
and what you want
to have happen
in your life."

Reflect

What is something you feel ashamed about? Could you flip your script?

_____
_____
_____
_____
_____
_____
_____
_____
_____
_____
_____
_____
_____
_____
_____
_____
_____
_____
_____
_____
_____
_____
_____
_____
_____
_____
_____
_____

"Do not feel ashamed
of who you are.
You have people in
your life who love
and support you just
exactly the way you
are right now."

Reflect

Name a recent dark time in your own life. How did you handle it?

_____
_____
_____
_____
_____
_____
_____
_____
_____
_____
_____
_____
_____
_____
_____
_____
_____
_____
_____
_____
_____
_____
_____
_____
_____
_____
_____
_____
_____

"In every dark time, there is a light. The best thing for us is to trust that everything will get better. Do not pin your life hopes on this time because things will change eventually. We just must pray for the best outcome and trust."

Reflect

What is one step you could take to overcome
your fear of discomfort and challenges?

_____
_____
_____
_____
_____
_____
_____
_____
_____
_____
_____
_____
_____
_____
_____
_____
_____
_____
_____
_____
_____
_____
_____
_____
_____
_____
_____

"Life is hard, but if you stop and look around you will see that you do hard things a lot! You just must believe that you can, and you will succeed."

What do you do when you are feeling lonely?

ASK
KATELYN

What do you do when you are feeling lonely?

I text a few friends or my aunties.

I schedule a FaceTime with my favorite people.

I write all my feelings down in my journal. Once it is outside of me, it does not feel so bad.

78

INSPIRATION

in·spi·ra·tion /
ˌinspəˈrāSH(ə)n/ noun

a sudden brilliant, creative, or timely idea; being stimulated to do or feel something, especially something creative.

QUOTES
ABOUT
INSPIRATION

Reflect

Do you notice a difference in your relationships
when you are more positive than negative?

_____
_____
_____
_____
_____
_____
_____
_____
_____
_____
_____
_____
_____
_____
_____
_____
_____
_____
_____
_____
_____
_____
_____
_____
_____
_____
_____
_____
_____
_____
_____

"Show your positive
and kindhearted
self to others and
they will love it!"

Reflect

What makes you unique? What are your special gifts?

_____
_____
_____
_____
_____
_____
_____
_____
_____
_____
_____
_____
_____
_____
_____
_____
_____
_____
_____
_____
_____
_____
_____
_____
_____
_____
_____

"Don't be afraid
to present your
sparkling and unique
self to the world."

Reflect

Are you mindful of other people's feelings?
When you are, does it make a difference?

"How you make others feel about themselves says a lot about you."

Reflect

Do you make time to find joy
every day? Brainstorm.

"Look for the most
beautiful thing
that touches your
heart today."

Reflect

List several ways you could think about
your current situation differently that
might change your way forward.

_____
_____
_____
_____
_____
_____
_____
_____
_____
_____
_____
_____
_____
_____
_____
_____
_____
_____
_____
_____
_____
_____
_____
_____
_____
_____
_____
_____

"The world we
create is based on
thoughts we think."

Reflect

What habits are you forming today that may impact your future? Evaluate it!

"The person that you choose to be is the person that you choose to become."

Reflect

Do you strive for perfection? What
would happen if you didn't?

_____
_____
_____
_____
_____
_____
_____
_____
_____
_____
_____
_____
_____
_____
_____
_____
_____
_____
_____
_____
_____
_____
_____
_____
_____
_____

"We are not perfect;
we are just unique and
that is all we can be."

Reflect

How do you show up in the world?
Do you lead with joy?

_____
_____
_____
_____
_____
_____
_____
_____
_____
_____
_____
_____
_____
_____
_____
_____
_____
_____
_____
_____
_____
_____
_____
_____
_____
_____
_____
_____

"Joy brings out the light inside of you. So be the one who shows joy to the world."

Reflect

Are you excluding anyone from your table?
Could you soften your heart and let them in?

_____
_____
_____
_____
_____
_____
_____
_____
_____
_____
_____
_____
_____
_____
_____
_____
_____
_____
_____
_____
_____
_____
_____
_____
_____
_____
_____

"No matter who you are, whether you have special needs or are different from other people, you are always invited to sit at my table."

(Inspired by Pastor Bob Mooney, Messiah

Lutheran Church, Yorba Linda, CA).

Reflect

Do your habits and work ethic attract success? Could you make a few changes to change the outcome?

_____
_____
_____
_____
_____
_____
_____
_____
_____
_____
_____
_____
_____
_____
_____
_____
_____
_____
_____
_____
_____
_____
_____
_____
_____
_____
_____
_____
_____
_____

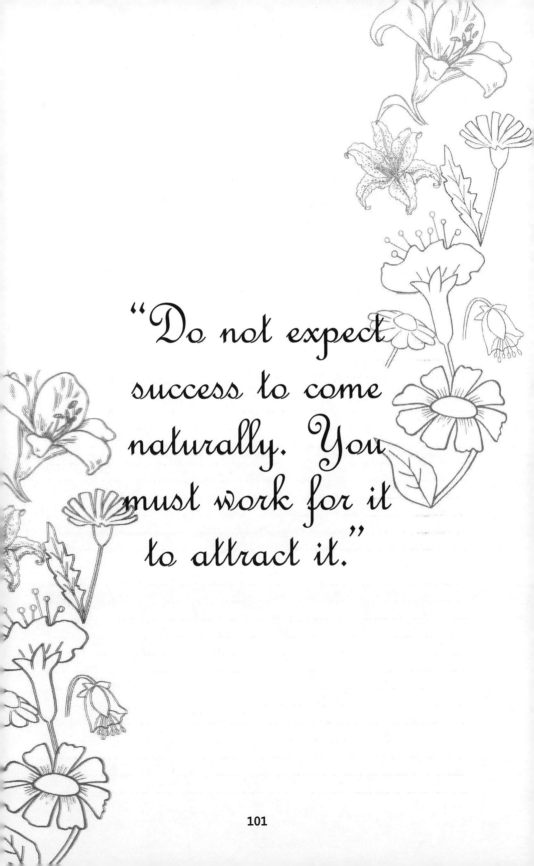

"Do not expect success to come naturally. You must work for it to attract it."

Reflect

In what special ways are you gifted? (Dig deep because sometimes we don't see our own gift).

_____
_____
_____
_____
_____
_____
_____
_____
_____
_____
_____
_____
_____
_____
_____
_____
_____
_____
_____
_____
_____
_____
_____
_____
_____
_____
_____
_____
_____
_____

"Being special does not make you a better person, it just means you are uniquely gifted in special ways."

Reflect

Do you ever let the world's loud voice override the deep love and knowing in your heart? Why?

_____
_____
_____
_____
_____
_____
_____
_____
_____
_____
_____
_____
_____
_____
_____
_____
_____
_____
_____
_____
_____
_____
_____
_____
_____
_____
_____
_____

"Your love inside
of you is stronger
than anything
around you."

Reflect

What is your truth? How can you live
your truth out loud in the world?

_____
_____
_____
_____
_____
_____
_____
_____
_____
_____
_____
_____
_____
_____
_____
_____
_____
_____
_____
_____
_____
_____
_____
_____
_____
_____
_____
_____
_____
_____

"Who you choose to become is up to you. The world does not revolve around you, but you revolve around the world. Speak your truth. It is yours and it is valuable."

Reflect

What can you give up doing that takes
time away from what you LOVE doing?

_____
_____
_____
_____
_____
_____
_____
_____
_____
_____
_____
_____
_____
_____
_____
_____
_____
_____
_____
_____
_____
_____
_____
_____
_____
_____
_____
_____

"You cannot be good at everything. Do not try to be like someone you are not. You have a unique offering to bring to the world."

Reflect

What might you try doing today if you knew your life may end in one year?

"Every moment of your life is a gift, so make the most of it and move forward now."

What do you do when you are feeling bored?

ASK
KATELYN

What do you do when you are feeling bored?

I grab my card making kit and customize a card for a friend or family member.

I get a bunch of magazines and cut out pictures that inspire me. I paste them to a big piece of construction paper while I listen to music.

I plan a movie marathon with a friend.

I watch a favorite show.

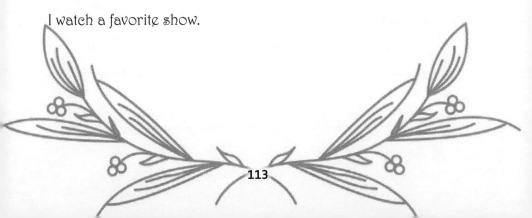

114

SELF-CARE

self-care /self/- /ker/ noun

The practice of taking an active role in protecting one's own well-being and happiness in mind, body, and spirit.

QUOTES ABOUT SELF-CARE

Reflect

What have you done and said just today?
What would you change?

_____
_____
_____
_____
_____
_____
_____
_____
_____
_____
_____
_____
_____
_____
_____
_____
_____
_____
_____
_____
_____
_____
_____
_____
_____
_____

"All you can control is what you do, what you say, and how you say it. That's all that matters."

Reflect

What can you do for yourself today that will feed your mind, body, and spirit?

_____
_____
_____
_____
_____
_____
_____
_____
_____
_____
_____
_____
_____
_____
_____
_____
_____
_____
_____
_____
_____
_____
_____
_____
_____
_____
_____

"Today is a great
day to stop and
ask yourself, "Am
I doing something
good for me?""

Reflect

Set your timer for 5 minutes and sit with your eyes closed in the silence. How did that feel? Could you do it more often?

_____
_____
_____
_____
_____
_____
_____
_____
_____
_____
_____
_____
_____
_____
_____
_____
_____
_____
_____
_____
_____
_____
_____
_____
_____

"Promise yourself to be strong and let nothing disturb your peace of mind."

Reflect

Does anxiety get in the way of your effectiveness? Who are YOUR trusted lifelines? List them.

_____
_____
_____
_____
_____
_____
_____
_____
_____
_____
_____
_____
_____
_____
_____
_____
_____
_____
_____
_____
_____
_____
_____
_____
_____
_____
_____
_____
_____

"Let your worries go. Figure out what you need to prepare for, and if you are feeling stressed, talk to someone you trust."

Reflect

Look at your habits, friends, job, etc.
What is one small change you can
make now, next week, next month?

_____
_____
_____
_____
_____
_____
_____
_____
_____
_____
_____
_____
_____
_____
_____
_____
_____
_____
_____
_____
_____
_____
_____
_____
_____
_____
_____
_____
_____
_____
_____

"It does not matter
if it is a relationship,
a lifestyle, or a job,
if it isn't making
you better and
happy, let it go."

Reflect

Do you speak up for yourself? Could you do it more? What is the worst that could happen?

_____
_____
_____
_____
_____
_____
_____
_____
_____
_____
_____
_____
_____
_____
_____
_____
_____
_____
_____
_____
_____
_____
_____
_____
_____
_____
_____

"If you see a problem happening, always be the one to speak up for yourself. Don't wait around for people to speak for you."

Reflect

What would you do and say if you had the courage to be truly you?

_____
_____
_____
_____
_____
_____
_____
_____
_____
_____
_____
_____
_____
_____
_____
_____
_____
_____
_____
_____
_____
_____
_____
_____
_____
_____
_____

"Don't try to be someone you are not. The person that you are today has a unique story to tell."

Reflect

What are the big and little things that make YOU happy?

"Do what makes you happy. Don't let others decide what that looks like for you."

Reflect

Make a list here of 10 things you are grateful for every day!

"If you have had a bad day and think that your life is terrible, think about what others don't have. Maybe that will make your day seem a little better."

Reflect

Set the timer for 10 minutes and just allow yourself to be in the silence. How did that feel different from 5 minutes of silence?

_____
_____
_____
_____
_____
_____
_____
_____
_____
_____
_____
_____
_____
_____
_____
_____
_____
_____
_____
_____
_____
_____
_____
_____
_____
_____
_____
_____
_____
_____
_____
_____

"Whatever you are doing, stop and be in the moment. Take some time out of your day to just sit down in peace and be alone with yourself."

Reflect

Do you compare yourself to others? Imagine here what your life would feel like if you didn't.

_____
_____
_____
_____
_____
_____
_____
_____
_____
_____
_____
_____
_____
_____
_____
_____
_____
_____
_____
_____
_____
_____
_____
_____
_____
_____
_____
_____
_____

"When you compare
yourself to others
it is a sign that
you do not like
yourself the way you
are. We all have
things we do best.
Everyone is different
and that is ok."

Reflect

Below, draw and color your very own STOP sign. The next time you are frustrated, remember this exercise: STOP, breath, and try again later.

_____
_____
_____
_____
_____
_____
_____
_____
_____
_____
_____
_____
_____
_____
_____
_____
_____
_____
_____
_____
_____
_____
_____
_____
_____
_____
_____

"Don't try so hard, beat yourself up, or get frustrated. The best thing you can do is walk away from it, breathe, and try again later."

Reflect

Do you rely on other people's opinions when making choices in your life? If so, why?

_____
_____
_____
_____
_____
_____
_____
_____
_____
_____
_____
_____
_____
_____
_____
_____
_____
_____
_____
_____
_____
_____
_____
_____
_____
_____
_____
_____
_____
_____
_____
_____

"When you decide to do something in life, stop and think to yourself, am I doing the right thing for me? If not, change it. If yes, never give up!"

Reflect

How can you take better care of your mind, body, and spirit? How might this change your life?

_____
_____
_____
_____
_____
_____
_____
_____
_____
_____
_____
_____
_____
_____
_____
_____
_____
_____
_____
_____
_____
_____
_____
_____
_____
_____
_____
_____

"We are all capable
of doing what is
right for ourselves.
So, whatever you do,
take care of yourself
and you will live a
much happier life."

What do you do to nurture yourself?

_____

_____

_____

_____

_____

_____

_____

_____

_____

_____

_____

_____

_____

_____

_____

_____

_____

_____

_____

_____

_____

ASK
KATELYN

What do you do to nurture yourself?

I take a hot shower.

I pick a day to stay in my pajamas all day.

I meditate using an app on my phone.

148

SELF-WORTH

self-worth /self/-/ wərTH/ noun

The internal sense of being good enough and worthy of love and belonging from others.

QUOTES ABOUT SELF-WORTH

Reflect

What is your superpower? If you
shared this gift with the people in
your life, what might happen?

"Be someone that finds their way, not someone who blocks the path."

Reflect

Have you ever said something in a hot moment that you regretted? How might that situation have been different had you stopped and thought first?

_____
_____
_____
_____
_____
_____
_____
_____
_____
_____
_____
_____
_____
_____
_____
_____
_____
_____
_____
_____
_____
_____
_____
_____
_____

"Anywhere you go, promise yourself to always stop before you speak."

Reflect

Does speaking up and speaking your truth scare you? Why? What is the worst thing that might happen if you said your truth?

_____
_____
_____
_____
_____
_____
_____
_____
_____
_____
_____
_____
_____
_____
_____
_____
_____
_____
_____
_____
_____
_____
_____
_____
_____
_____
_____
_____
_____

"Let your voice be heard. Do not let others speak for you."

Reflect

What would happen if you took your choices into your own hands?

_____
_____
_____
_____
_____
_____
_____
_____
_____
_____
_____
_____
_____
_____
_____
_____
_____
_____
_____
_____
_____
_____
_____
_____
_____
_____
_____
_____
_____
_____

"Everything you do in life is an opportunity for you to make a choice all your own."

Reflect

Do the people in your life support and reflect your best self?

_____
_____
_____
_____
_____
_____
_____
_____
_____
_____
_____
_____
_____
_____
_____
_____
_____
_____
_____
_____
_____
_____
_____
_____
_____
_____
_____

"The people you feel most connected to are the ones you should surround yourself with."

Reflect

In what ways are you enough? List 5.

"Believe that you are enough because that is what matters most!"

Reflect

What are you really feeling today,
deep down? Can you let it out?

_____
_____
_____
_____
_____
_____
_____
_____
_____
_____
_____
_____
_____
_____
_____
_____
_____
_____
_____
_____
_____
_____
_____
_____
_____
_____
_____
_____

"Allow the emotion you are feeling right now, even if your feelings are deep. Then, let it shine from the bottom up! Don't let anything get in the way of you being the best you!"

Reflect

Can you imagine a future where your difference is your strength? Dream it and write it here.

_____
_____
_____
_____
_____
_____
_____
_____
_____
_____
_____
_____
_____
_____
_____
_____
_____
_____
_____
_____
_____
_____
_____

"Everywhere you go, you will find people that look totally different from you. And that is ok! You don't have to look exactly like them to fit in or to be popular. You are your own unique and beautiful self."

Reflect

How can you nurture and challenge
yourself toward your personal dreams?

"Do not doubt the person you are. Just keep nurturing and challenging yourself and you will succeed in life."

Reflect

Why are popularity and people pleasing so desirable? What could you accomplish if you did not have to worry about that anymore?

_____
_____
_____
_____
_____
_____
_____
_____
_____
_____
_____
_____
_____
_____
_____
_____
_____
_____
_____
_____
_____
_____
_____
_____
_____
_____
_____
_____

"If you think being popular will make you a better person, think again. You are different from everyone else; you are unique and that is the most important thing to be."

Reflect

What do you have the confidence and
desire to do in your lifetime?

_____
_____
_____
_____
_____
_____
_____
_____
_____
_____
_____
_____
_____
_____
_____
_____
_____
_____
_____
_____
_____
_____
_____
_____
_____
_____
_____
_____
_____

"If you feel different from others, it means you have a special power for doing things that other people may not have the confidence to do."

Reflect

How can you turn off the opinions
of others and tune into your own
unique voice, ideas, and plans?

_____
_____
_____
_____
_____
_____
_____
_____
_____
_____
_____
_____
_____
_____
_____
_____
_____
_____
_____
_____
_____
_____
_____
_____
_____
_____
_____
_____
_____
_____
_____

"Do not let criticism get in the way of being true to yourself. People may see you in a different way than you see yourself, but that is their problem."

Reflect

What would it take to approve of yourself as you are, right now, in this moment?

"When you accept yourself for exactly who you are, it means you like the way you are in this moment."

Reflect

How would your life be different if you
always chose what was best for you?

_____
_____
_____
_____
_____
_____
_____
_____
_____
_____
_____
_____
_____
_____
_____
_____
_____
_____
_____
_____
_____
_____
_____
_____
_____
_____
_____

"If you had to choose between being true to yourself or denying who you are, always choose being true! You never know how life is going to treat you, but if you know who you are and like who you are, you will likely become the very best version of yourself."

What do you do when you are feeling sad or overwhelmed?

_____

_____

_____

_____

_____

_____

_____

_____

_____

_____

_____

_____

_____

_____

_____

_____

_____

_____

ASK
KATELYN

What do you do when you are feeling sad or overwhelmed?

I try to think about what I am grateful for and write at least 5 things in my journal. If you can do it every day, it really changes what you focus on.

I go into my room, close the door and cry. It is ok to cry and allow yourself to be sad. Then I come out of my room and spend time with my family. It may not solve my problem, but it sure helps.

I write quotes! I also write poems. They help me to get my inside feelings out. And it helps me know how to organize my thoughts for the next day.

Wisdom for Your Journey

The Lotus Mandala on the previous page was created by artist Elizabeth Buchter, the creator of all the custom mandalas in this journal.

A mandala is a geometric figure that represents the universe in both Hindu and Buddhist symbolism. It reflects a dreamer's search for completeness, self-unity, and the balance of mind, body, and spirit.

The lotus flowers represented inside this mandala represent purity, enlightenment, self-renewal, and rebirth.

In this next section, may these ideas help you to go inward and reflect more deeply as you pour out your own wisdom for your unique journey.

My Wisdom for
my Journey

Created by:

_____

_____

Today, I am thinking about . . .

Today, I am thinking about . . .

_____
_____
_____
_____
_____
_____
_____
_____
_____
_____
_____
_____
_____
_____
_____
_____
_____
_____
_____
_____
_____
_____
_____
_____
_____
_____
_____

Today, I am thinking about . . .

Today, I am thinking about . . .

Today, I am thinking about . . .

Today, I am thinking about . . .

Today, I am thinking about . . .

Today, I am thinking about . . .

Today, I am thinking about . . .

Today, I am thinking about . . .

Today, I am thinking about . . .

Today, I am thinking about . . .

Today, I am thinking about . . .

Today, I am thinking about . . .

Today, I am thinking about . . .

Today, I am thinking about . . .

Today, I am thinking about . . .

Q & A with Katelyn Reed

Why did you start writing your own quotes?

I started writing my own quotes because I was feeling alone and sad. My quote writing helped me focus on my thoughts and feelings and helped me know how I wanted to feel. I realized at some point that most everyone feels like I do. My quotes have ended up helping me, and other people, too.

Why did you start writing your quotes every night before you went to bed?

Because the nighttime is a place and a time to open myself up, to pour my heart out from that day, and to remember what I learned, remember something I saw, a good thing that captured me. It helped me to have some peace at night.

How did the quote writing help to prepare you for the next day?

It helped me figure out how much effort I should put into the next day and where to spend my time and energy. I want to show people that it is ok to just be yourself and to feel your own feelings. My quotes helped me to create a new mini chapter for my life each day.

Why did you decide to put your quotes in a book and why did you pick a journal format?

I chose this format because I want to inspire people to be the best they can be. I want to provide my readers with a place to pour out their heart, their feelings, and to connect with their own ideas about their life and how they affect other people. I also wanted to share my own tips and ideas for how to get rid of stress in a fun and interactive way.

Why did you decide to add the journal question prompts?

The journal prompts allow the reader to understand my perspective and then have their own chance to think about their opinions and express their own personal views on life.

Why did you add the mandala artwork and coloring aspect to your journal?

I added the coloring because it balances the journaling. When you journal, you express a lot of emotion that moves through your body. Coloring is a fun and relaxing way to ease into the emotion, to color it out, and to get it out of your head. The words help you feel; the coloring helps you to let it all go.

Why do you like to color?

I love to color! It helps me relax. I color when I am stressed, for fun, or when I want to be inspired. I color with my favorite music in my ear.

What are some other activities you do when you are feeling stressed, sad, or worried?

I like to meditate. I notice when I am stressed or when I get myself all worked up over little things, I like to go into my room, close the door, lay down, and meditate. I like to listen to inspirational music like the Beatles and music that makes me happy. I love to dance, too. It is a great way to let your feelings go. When I watch dance shows or dance movies, they dance with and through their emotion. Dance helps to express and release all the feelings in your body.

If you had to give a message to your readers?

Don't let yourself get worked up in any situation because it is not worth it. I have felt it a lot before. It is not good to doubt yourself or shut down your emotions. It is healthy to let those emotions out somehow, in a way that is not hurting you but allowing the feelings to pass through and out.

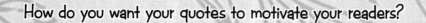

How do you want your quotes to motivate your readers?

I want to motivate my readers to express their feelings more. I write a lot about how to work through stress, how to find the brighter side, how to feel better about the unique person you are. We all have lots of worries and on these pages, we can learn to understand our feelings and let go of the ones that don't help us.

PHOTO GALLERY

Katelyn as young "Adelaide" in American Horror Story. On location in Los Angeles, CA, 2011

Katelyn in the role of "Pepper" with "Sandy" the dog in a MFAM production of Little Orphan Annie, 2018.

Katelyn as "Annie" and her dad as "Daddy
Warbucks." Halloween, 2009.

Katelyn in Key West, Florida swimming with dolphins, 2016

Katelyn as "Gracie" on the set of Good Luck Charlie.
Sunset Bronson Studios, Los Angeles, CA, 2012.

Katelyn with Mr. Andrew Babbitt; counselor, mentor, and the inspiration for Wisdom from The Whiteboard.

The beginning of Katelyn's passion for Show Choir. Brea Junior High, Brea, CA 2016.

Katelyn learning to snow ski at age 5.
Mammoth Lakes, CA 2008.

Katelyn as "Sister Bertha" in a Center Stage production
of Sound of Music. Yorba Linda, CA, 2019.

Show Choir Competition, 2019. Tiffanys takes
1st place! Los Angeles, CA, 2019.

Katelyn with Master Kwon at her Tae Kwon Do
Black Belt Ceremony. Brea, CA, 2017

Katelyn with her biggest fans. Mammoth Lakes, CA, 2007.

Acknowledgements

Mom and Dad, Grammy & Papa Robb, Grandma and Grandpa Reed, Aunt Cindy Reed, Aunt Alison Buchter and The Buchter Family, and Beatrice "Oma" Gulden. Gary Kain, Barbara Basalone, and all of my Olinda Village family, my dear friends who feel like family, and the super amazing Chromie Crew!

Alisha Freeman-Rembert who gave me the courage, research, and inspiration to pursue this project.

EIP (Early Intervention Program, Laguna Beach, CA). ICEC (Intervention Center for Early Childhood, Santa Ana, CA). Mrs. Brown at Mrs. Brown's House. BOUSD (Brea Olinda Unified School District): Andrew Babbitt, Sonia Kadakia, Kelly Kennedy, Jeanine Leach, Lauri Maddock, Kerry Mamrot, Kristen Risberg, Melissa Stahly, Trina Starke, John Thorsen, Stacy Yoder, and all the wonderful teachers who encouraged me. Gail Williamson at KMR Talent. Master Kwon, Master Jasmine, and Master Thomas of TKD Masters, Brea, CA. DSES (Disabled Skiers of the Eastern Sierra, Mammoth Lakes, CA).

A special shout out to all the speech therapists, physical therapists, psychologists, and Regional Center social workers who have worked diligently with me my whole life to ensure that I have access to all the programs and services that I need to be the best me I can be.